A Stirling Le-Moo Story

Dopple Brook Zoo

By Valerie M Cootes

Illustrated by Sonia M White

Sonia White Publisher

Dopple Brook Zoo: A Stirling Le-Moo Story
By Valerie M. Cootes
ISBN 9780994109705

Sonia White Publisher
19 Sharon Road, Waiake
Auckland 0630
New Zealand
Sonia@giftedconsultant.ac.nz

Poor Stirling Le-Moo

Didn't know what to do,

So he decided to go to the Zoo.

Then without any fuss, he got on the green bus,

And set off for Dopple Brook Zoo.

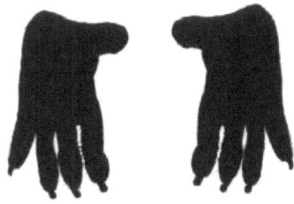

And who did he meet at the zoo?

A Lion roared "Boo!"

And "How do you do?"

"Would you like some meat to chew?"

"No, thank you!" said Moo,

 "I've a lot to do.

I'm off to explore the Zoo."

A Brown Bear growled "Boo!"

And "How do you do?"

"Would you like some sweet honey too?"

"No, thank you!" said Moo,

"I've a lot to do.

I'm off to explore the Zoo."

A giraffe murmured "Boo!"

And "How do you do?"

"Would you like some

green leaves too?"

"No, thank you!" said Moo,

"I've a lot to do."

"I'm off to explore the Zoo."

An Elephant trumpeted "Boo!"

And "How do you do?"

"Would you like a sticky bun too?"

"No, thank you!" said Moo,

"I've a lot to do.

I'm off to explore the Zoo."

The meerkats yapped "Boo!"

And "How do you do?"

"Would you like some fat spiders too?"

"No, thank you!" said Moo,

"I've a lot to do.

I'm off to explore the Zoo."

A camel moaned "Boo!"

And

"How do you do?"

"Would you like some juicy dates, too?"

"No, thank you!" said Moo,

"I've a lot to do.

I'm off to explore the Zoo."

A monkey shrieked

"Boo!"

And "How do you do?"

"Would you like some

peanuts, too?"

"No, thank you!" said Moo,
"I've a lot to do.

I'm off to explore the Zoo."

A seal barked "Boo!"

And "How do you do?"

"Would you like some silver fish too?"

"No, thank you!" said Moo,

"I've a lot to do.

"I'm off to explore the Zoo."

A little girl sobbed "Boo!"

"I've lost my red shoe."

"Where can I find it? Boo hoo!"

"I'm sorry" said Moo,

"I haven't a clue

Where to find your little red shoe."

"Now, what do I do

To make my way through

To the gates of this wonderful Zoo?"

But without any fuss,

He found the green bus

And rode home from Dopple Brook Zoo.

www.ingramcontent.com/pod-product-compliance
Lightning Source LLC
LaVergne TN
LVHW072122070426
835511LV00002B/69